GRADES K–1

SCHOLASTIC

LITTLE LEARNER PACKETS

SIGHT WORDS

Violet Findley

Cover design: Tannaz Fassihi; Cover illustration: Jason Dove
Interior design: Michelle H. Kim
Interior illustration: Doug Jones

ISBN: 978-1-338-22827-4
Copyright © 2018 by Scholastic Inc.
All rights reserved.
Printed in the U.S.A.
First printing, January 2018.

1 2 3 4 5 6 7 8 9 10   40   24 23 22 21 20 19 18

Table of Contents

Introduction

Reading specialists have long agreed that a mastery of sight words is the golden key to unlocking reading confidence and agility. But how do busy educators find the time to help children commit all of these tricky words to memory? Welcome to *Little Learner Packets: Sight Words*! The 10 learning packets in this book provide fun, playful activities that teach and reinforce the top 40 high-frequency words in print. (See the Top 40 Sight Words box.)

Each packet invites children to read, trace, write, graph, match, find, unscramble, and review four key sight words to make learning stick! You can use the packets in a variety of ways and with children of all learning styles. Children can complete the activities at their seats or in a learning center. They can also use the pages as take-home practice. The packets are ideal for encouraging children to work independently and at their own pace. A grid on the introduction page of each packet lets children track their progress as they complete each page. Best of all, the activities support children in meeting the standards for Reading Foundational Skills for Kindergarten. (See the Connections to the Standards box.)

Top 40 Sight Words

PACKET 1: is, a, of, in

PACKET 2: and, the, to, you

PACKET 3: that, it, he, was

PACKET 4: she, for, are, as

PACKET 5: I, on, they, with

PACKET 6: be, at, have, this

PACKET 7: had, from, we, or

PACKET 8: said, words, not, what

PACKET 9: all, were, can, by

PACKET 10: but, one, when, your

How to Use the Sight-Word Packets

Copy a class supply of the eight pages for the sight-word packet you want to use. Then sequence and staple each set of pages together and distribute the packets to children. All they need to complete the pages are pencils and crayons. TIP: To save paper, we suggest you make double-sided copies.

The format of the learning packets makes the pages easy to use. Here's what you'll find on each page:

Page 1 / Introduction: This page introduces the four sight words that are featured in the packet. Children trace and write the words on the page. When the activity is finished, children color in the first box in the tracking grid at the bottom. As they complete each of the remaining pages in the packet, children will color in the corresponding box in this grid.

Pages 2 & 3 / Read & Write: First, children read the illustrated "story sentence" that presents the featured sight words in context. They then practice writing the sight words to promote automaticity and handwriting skills.

Page 4 / Color: At the top of this page, a color code is provided for children to use to color the picture. The activity provides an engaging way to reinforce the featured sight words while giving kids important practice in fine-motor skills and following directions.

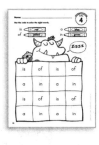

Page 5 / Graph: The activity gives children the opportunity to reinforce sight-word knowledge as they boost early math skills by graphing the four featured sight words. TIP: Invite children to discuss their results by taking a quick look at the graph.

Page 6 / Match & Find: At the top of the page, children draw lines to match each of the featured sight words. At the bottom of the page, children locate each sight word in a simple hidden-word puzzle. NOTE: Each sight word appears in the puzzle once, horizontally.

Page 7 / Unscramble: This entertaining page provides additional practice by challenging children to unscramble and write each sight word two times.

Page 8 / Review: Children complete a humorous, illustrated story by writing each sight word in the appropriate blank. At the bottom of the page, children can "close out" the packet by identifying the four featured sight words one last time. TIP: When the blanks are filled in, you can boost early literacy skills by running your finger under the text and reading the story aloud together.

Answer Key: A handy answer key is provided on pages 87–96. The thumbnail images allow you to check children's completed pages at a glance. You can then use the results to determine areas in which they might need additional instruction or practice.

Teaching Tips

Use these tips to help children get the most from the learning packets.

★ **Provide a model:** Demonstrate, step by step, how to complete each page in the first packet. Children should then be able to complete the remaining packets independently.

★ **Focus on the target words:** Have children identify each target sight word and finger-write it in the air. You can also work together to craft simple sentences that include the sight words. After they're written, read them aloud together!

★ **Offer additional practice:** Play sight-word games! For example: Write each sight word on two index cards. Shuffle the cards and place them facedown, challenging children to turn over the cards and make matches.

Learning Centers

You might label a separate folder with each child's name and place the packets in the folder to keep in a learning center. Then children can retrieve the assigned packet and work independently through the pages during center time. To make the packets self-checking, you can enlarge the answer keys for each packet, cut apart the images, then sequence and staple them together to create a mini answer key for that packet. Finally, place all of the answer keys in the center. Children can check their completed pages by referring to the corresponding answer key.

Ways to Use the Sight-Word Learning Packets

Children can work through the packets at their own pace, tracking their progress as they complete each page. The packets are ideal for the following:

★ Learning center activity

★ Independent seatwork

★ One-on-one lesson

★ Morning starter

★ End of the day wrap-up

★ Take-home practice

Assessing Learning

Let's learn sight words!

To quickly assess children's sight word recognition skills, do the following:

★ Display each sight word and have children read it aloud.

★ Call out each sight word and have children write it down.

★ Call out each sight word and challenge children to use it in a sentence. TIP: Younger students can say the sentences. Older students can write the sentences.

★ Reteach sight words that individual children are struggling with to hardwire memorization.

Name: _____

SIGHT WORDS
is, a, of, in

Hi!

is

a

of

in

Write the words above. Color in each box when you complete an activity.

1 Introduction	**2** Read & Write	**3** Read & Write	**4** Color
5 Graph	**6** Match & Find	**7** Unscramble	**8** Review

Name: _____

Read the sentence.

The monster **is** playing with **a** friend.

Write the sight words.

is

is

a

a

Name: _____

Read the sentence.

There are lots **of** socks **in** the monster soup.

Write the sight words.

of

in

Little Learner Packets: Sight Words © Scholastic Inc.

Name: _____

Use the code to color the sight words.

is — red
of — yellow

a — blue
in — green

Zzzz

is	of	is	of
a	in	a	in
is	of	is	of
a	in	a	in

Name: _____

Count and graph the sight words.

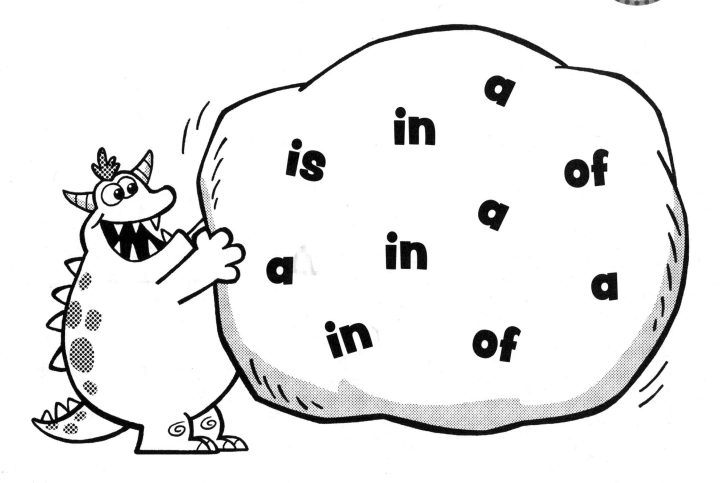

	is	a	of	in
4				
3				
2				
1				

Name: _____

Draw lines to match the sight words.

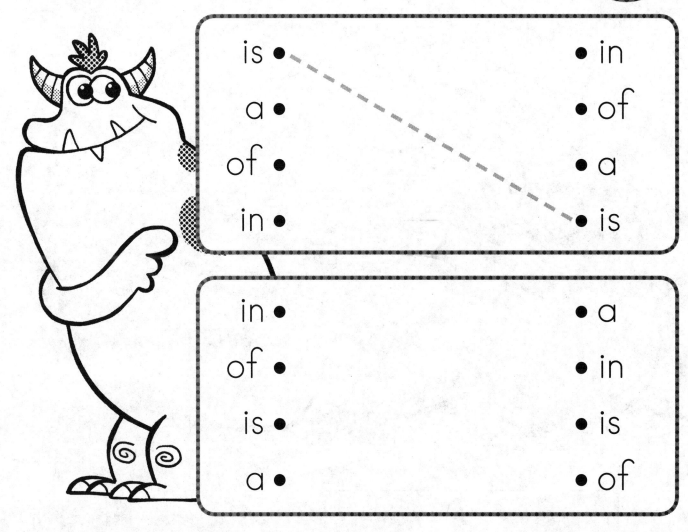

is •   • in

a •   • of

of •   • a

in •   • is

in •   • a

of •   • in

is •   • is

a •   • of

Circle each sight word from the Word Bank once.

h g a d x q u m

p b i s u c w v

c g z e k r o f

k u g i n v f w

Word Bank

is a of in

Name: _____

Unscramble each sight word.

is   a   of   in

si _____

fo _____

a _____

ni _____

a _____

fo _____

si _____

ni _____

Name: _____

Word Bank

is
a
of
in

Use each sight word once to complete the story. Then read it aloud.

Here is _____ monster.

He has a bowl _____ soup.

He is _____ a house with a pal.

He _____ so happy.

Bye! Great work!

Color the boxes with the four sight words you learned in this packet.

is	we	the	of
you	a	in	to

14

Name: _____

SIGHT WORDS
and, the, to, you

Hi!

and
the
to
you

Write the words above. Color in each box when you complete an activity.

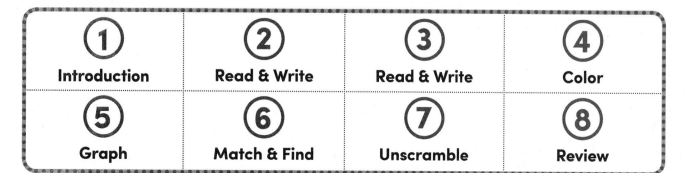

① **Introduction**	② **Read & Write**	③ **Read & Write**	④ **Color**
⑤ **Graph**	⑥ **Match & Find**	⑦ **Unscramble**	⑧ **Review**

Name: _____

Read the sentence.

The bear and the monster are best friends.

Write the sight words.

and

and

the

the

Name: _____

Read the sentence.

"I have a gift **to** give **you**!" said the monster.

Write the sight words.

to	you

Name: _____

Use the code to color the sight words.

and red   the blue

to yellow   you green

Zzzz

and	the	you	the
to	and	to	you
and	the	and	you
to	you	to	the

Name: _____

Count and graph the sight words.

	and	the	to	you
4				
3				
2				
1				

Little Learner Packets: Sight Words © Scholastic Inc.

Name: _____

Draw lines to match the sight words.

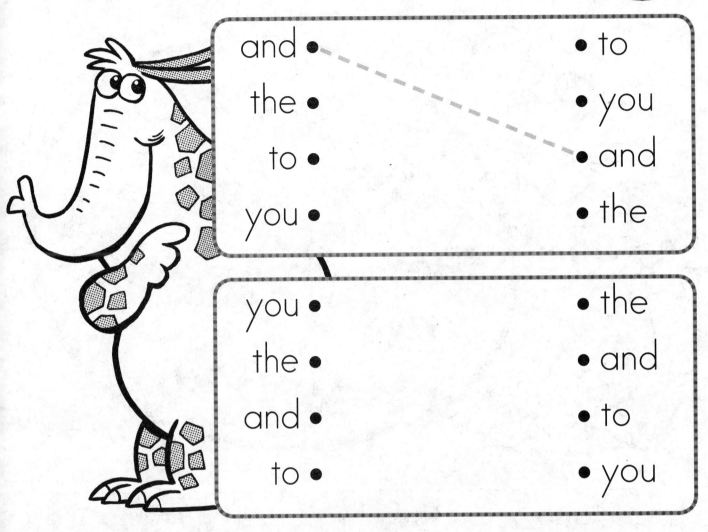

and •　　　　　• to

the •　　　　　• you

to •　　　　　• and

you •　　　　　• the

you •　　　　　• the

the •　　　　　• and

and •　　　　　• to

to •　　　　　• you

Circle each sight word from the Word Bank once.

p d t h e g w a

f y z e t o s f

n c y o u x p t

n x a n d v i p

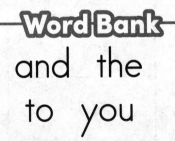

Word Bank

and　the
to　you

20

Little Learner Packets: Sight Words © Scholastic Inc.

Name: _____

Unscramble each sight word.

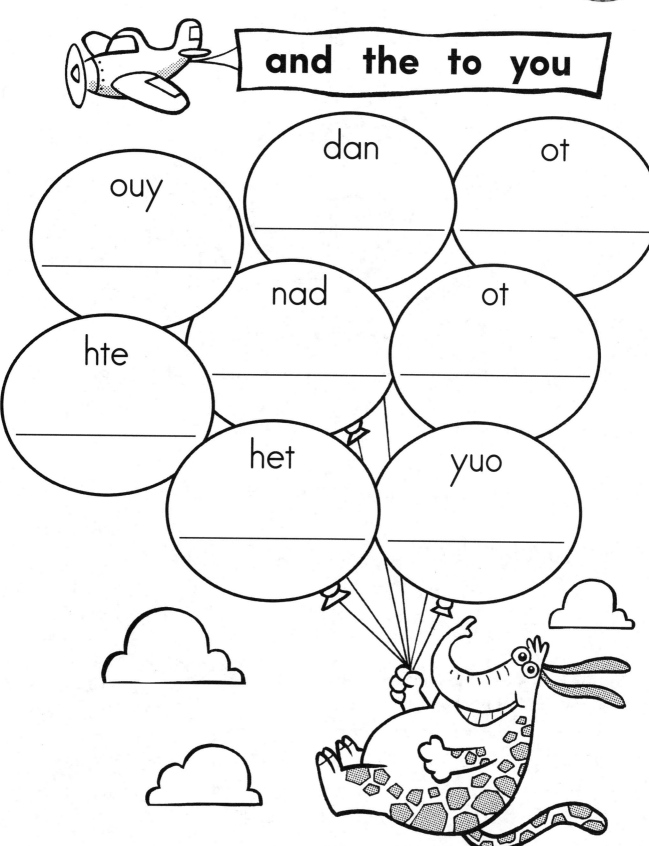

and   the   to   you

ouy
_____

dan
_____

ot
_____

hte
_____

nad
_____

ot
_____

het
_____

yuo
_____

Word Bank

and

the

to

you

Use each sight word once to complete the story. Then read it aloud.

See the monster _____ the bear.

They went _____ the park.

The monster is on _____ swing.

"Will _____ push me?" he asked the bear.

Color the boxes with the four sight words you learned in this packet.

and	or	the	be
I	to	he	you

BYE! GREAT WORK!

22

Name: _____

SIGHT WORDS
that, it, he, was

Hi!

that	that
it	it
he	he
was	was

Write the words above. Color in each box when you complete an activity.

① Introduction	② Read & Write	③ Read & Write	④ Color
⑤ Graph	⑥ Match & Find	⑦ Unscramble	⑧ Review

Name: _____

Read the sentence.

The monster was sad <u>**that**</u> <u>**it**</u> was raining.

Write the sight words.

that

it

Name: _____

Read the sentence.

The sun came out, and <u>**he was**</u> happy!

Write the sight words.

he

was

Name: _____

Use the code to color the sight words.

that — red
he — yellow

it — blue
was — green

he	was	he	was
that	it	was	it
he	was	it	that
that	he	that	it

Zzzz

Little Learner Packets: Sight Words © Scholastic Inc.

Name: _____

Count and graph the sight words.

	that	it	he	was
4				
3				
2				
1				

Name: _____

Draw lines to match the sight words.

that •　　　• was

it •　　　• he

he •　　　• it

was •　　　• that

that •　　　• was

it •　　　• he

he •　　　• it

was •　　　• that

Circle each sight word from the Word Bank once.

z p x w a s o d

u r h e c f p w

d g y i t n j v

o t h a t g k j

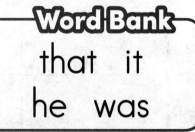

Word Bank

that　it

he　was

Little Learner Packets: Sight Words © Scholastic Inc.

SIGHT WORDS 3
Unscramble
7

Name: ______________________________

Unscramble each sight word.

that it he was

hatt ______________

ti ______________

eh ______________

aws ______________

eh ______________

saw ______________

atth ______________

ti ______________

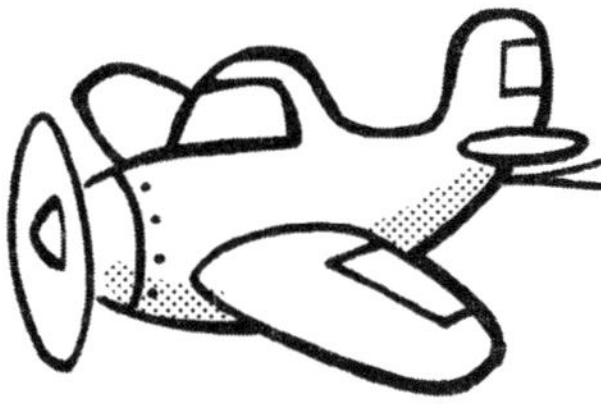

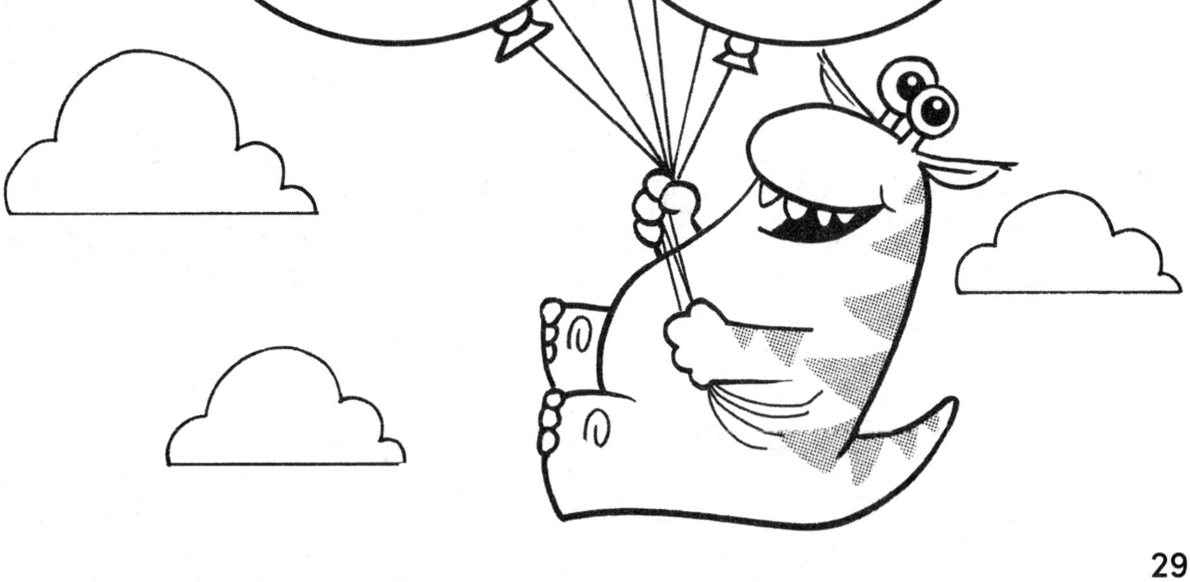

Name: _____

that

it

he

was

Use each sight word once to complete the story. Then read it aloud.

The monster _____ at the beach.

He saw _____ big fish.

He saw _____ jump up and wave.

So _____ said, "Hello, big fish!"

Color the boxes with the four sight words you learned in this packet.

not	it	the	that
was	he	can	said

30

Name: _____

Hi!

SIGHT WORDS
she, for, are, as

she | she _____
for | for _____
are | are _____
as | as _____

Write the words above. Color in each box when you complete an activity.

① Introduction	② Read & Write	③ Read & Write	④ Color
⑤ Graph	⑥ Match & Find	⑦ Unscramble	⑧ Review

Little Learner Packets: Sight Words © Scholastic Inc.

Name: _____

Read the sentence.

Look, <u>**she**</u> has a teddy bear <u>**for**</u> the baby!

Write the sight words.

she

for

Little Learner Packets: Sight Words © Scholastic Inc.

Name: _____

Read the sentence.

The cats **are** **as** sleepy **as** the baby monster.

Write the sight words.

are

as

Use the code to color the sight words.

she — red
are — yellow

for — blue
as — green

are	as	for	as
she	for	she	are
she	are	as	as
are	for	she	for

Little Learner Packets: Sight Words © Scholastic Inc.

Name: _____Count and graph the sight words.

	she	for	are	as
4				
3				
2				
1				

Name: _____

Draw lines to match the sight words.

she •	• for
for •	• as
are •	• are
as •	• she

as •	• as
are •	• for
for •	• she
she •	• are

Circle each sight word from the Word Bank once.

t g s h e b v o

v u f o r n g m

r u c d a s r i

c o p o t a r e

Word Bank

she   for
are   as

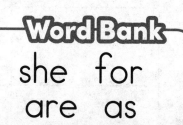

Name: _____

Unscramble each sight word.

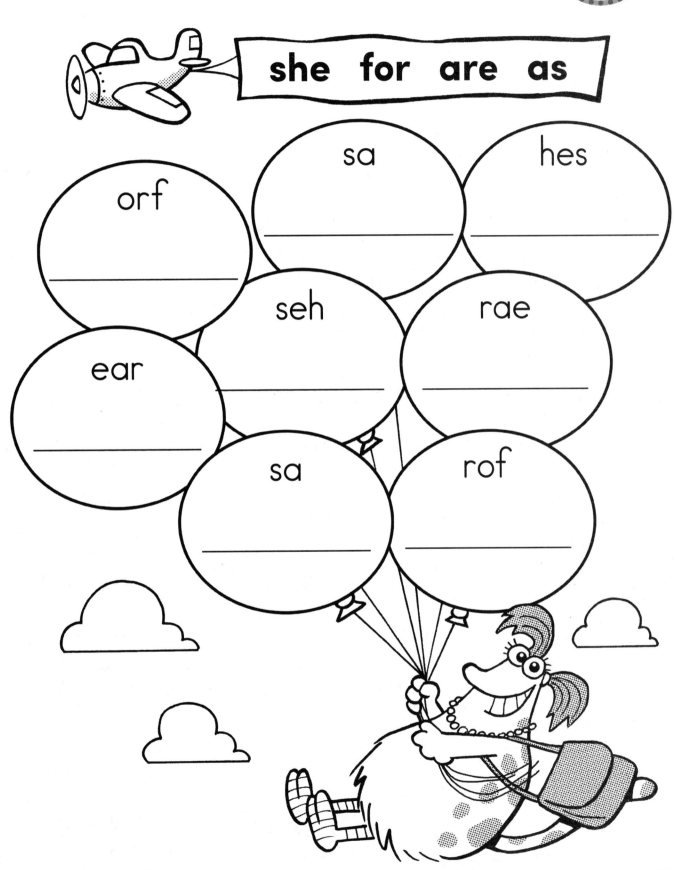

she for are as

orf
_____

sa
_____

hes
_____

seh
_____

rae
_____

ear
_____

sa
_____

rof
_____

Name: _____

Word Bank

she

for

are

as

Use each sight word once to complete the story. Then read it aloud.

Here _____ two nice monsters.

He is a baby, and _____ is a mom.

She has a bottle _____ the baby.

He is _____ happy as can be!

**Color the boxes with the four sight words
you learned in this packet.**

a	for	by	are
is	as	said	she

BYE!
GREAT
JOB!

Little Learner Packets: Sight Words © Scholastic Inc.

38

Name: _____

SIGHT WORDS
I, on, they, with

Hi!

I   I _____
_____

on   on _____
_____

they they _____
_____

with with _____

Write the words above. Color in each box when you complete an activity.

① Introduction	② Read & Write	③ Read & Write	④ Color
⑤ Graph	⑥ Match & Find	⑦ Unscramble	⑧ Review

Name: _____

Read the sentence.

"**I** am **on** top of the mountain!"
said the monster.

Write the sight words.

I

on

Little Learner Packets: Sight Words © Scholastic Inc.

Name: _____

Read the sentence.

"I am happy **they** are here **with** me!"
said the monster.

Write the sight words.

they	with

Name: _____

Use the code to color the sight words.

I — red

they — yellow

on — blue

with — green

Zzzz

with	they	I	they
they	I	on	I
I	on	with	they
on	with	on	with

Name: _____

Count and graph the sight words.

	I	**on**	**they**	**with**
4				
3				
2				
1				

Name: _____

Draw lines to match the sight words.

I •   • on

on •   • with

they •   • they

with •   • I

with •   • on

on •   • I

I •   • with

they •   • they

Circle each sight word from the Word Bank once.

b w I t h p a c

s a t h e y u w

h I x o n y a v

b c a l w i t h

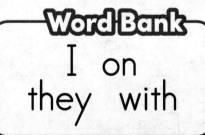

Word Bank

I   on
they   with

Name: _____

Unscramble each sight word.

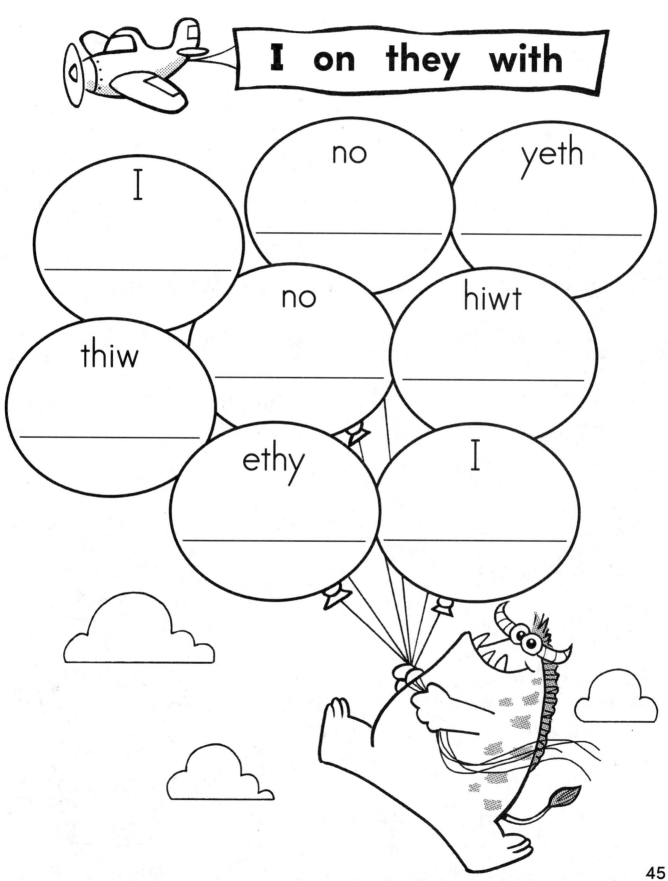

I on they with

no

yeth

I _____

no _____

hiwt _____

thiw _____

ethy _____

I _____

Name: _____

SIGHT WORDS 5
Review
8

Word Bank

I

on

they

with

Use each sight word once to complete the story. Then read it aloud.

The pals put _____ their skates.

Then _____ skated on the lake.

"_____ like to skate with you!"
said the monster.

"We like to skate _____ you, too!"
said the penguins.

**Color the boxes with the four sight words
you learned in this packet.**

I	said	a	with
all	on	they	he

BYE!
GREAT
JOB!

46

Little Learner Packets: Sight Words © Scholastic Inc.

Name: _____

SIGHT WORDS
be, at, have, this

be   be
at   at
have have
this this

Hi!

Write the words above. Color in each box when you complete an activity.

①	②	③	④
Introduction	**Read & Write**	**Read & Write**	**Color**
⑤	⑥	⑦	⑧
Graph	**Match & Find**	**Unscramble**	**Review**

Name: _____

Read the sentence.

The monster loves to **be** **at** the hat shop!

Write the sight words.

be	at

Name: _____

Read the sentence.

"I <u>**have**</u> to try on <u>**this**</u> tall hat!" said the monster.

Write the sight words.

have

this

Name: _____

Use the code to color the sight words.

be 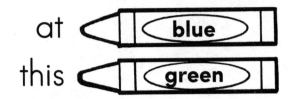 red

have yellow

at blue

this green

have	this	have	this
be	at	at	be
have	this	at	have
be	at	be	this

Name: _____

Count and graph the sight words.

	be	at	have	this
4				
3				
2				
1				

Little Learner Packets: Sight Words © Scholastic Inc.

Name: _____

Draw lines to match the sight words.

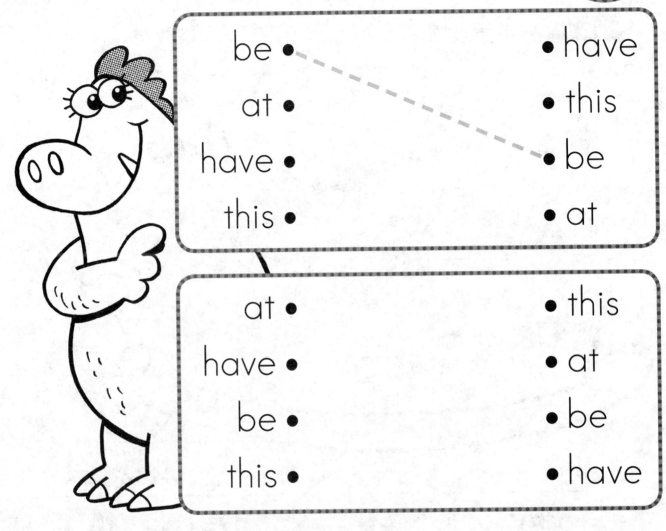

be •   • have

at •   • this

have •   • be

this •   • at

at •   • this

have •   • at

be •   • be

this •   • have

Circle each sight word from the Word Bank once.

m u h a v e t h

f l o c b e o y

u x t h i s m n

w z a t i r a h

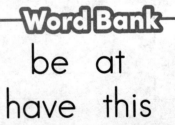

Word Bank

be   at
have   this

Unscramble each sight word.

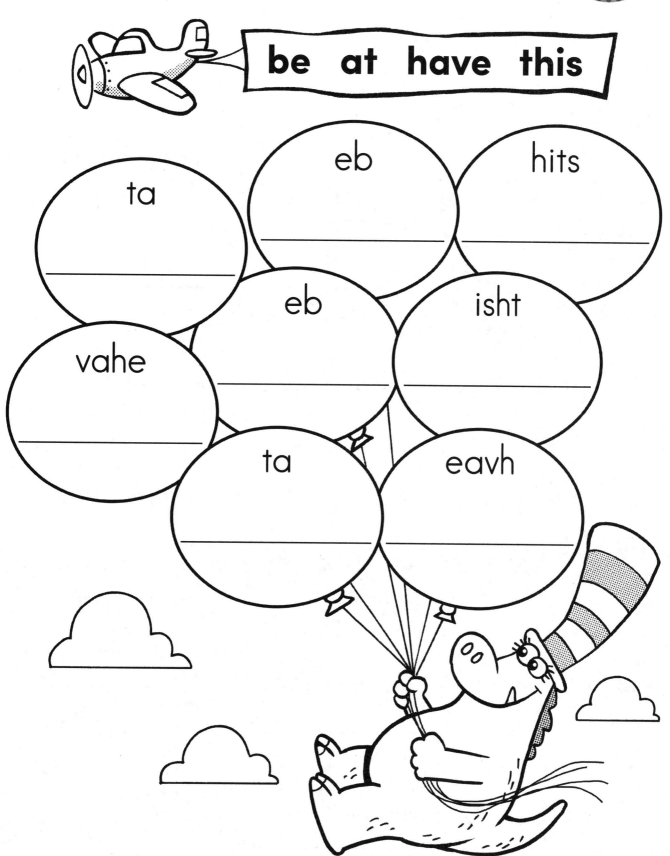

be at have this

ta

eb

hits

vahe

eb

isht

ta

eavh

Word Bank

be
at
have
this

Use each sight word once to complete the story. Then read it aloud.

The monster was _____ the hat shop.

She put on _____ nice hat with dots.

The hat made her as happy as can _____.

"I must _____ it!" she said.

Color the boxes with the four sight words you learned in this packet.

be	and	on	at
the	this	have	is

BYE! GREAT JOB!

54

Name: _____

SIGHT WORDS
had, from, we, or

Hi!

had   had
from   from
we   we
or   or

Write the words above. Color in each box when you complete an activity.

① Introduction	② Read & Write	③ Read & Write	④ Color
⑤ Graph	⑥ Match & Find	⑦ Unscramble	⑧ Review

Name: _____

Read the sentence.

The monster **had** a pal **from** Mars.

Write the sight words.

had

from

Name: _____

Read the sentence.

The monster said, "Should <u>we</u> play with the car <u>or</u> the ball?"

Write the sight words.

we	or

Little Learner Packets: Sight Words © Scholastic Inc.

Name: _____

Use the code to color the sight words.

had 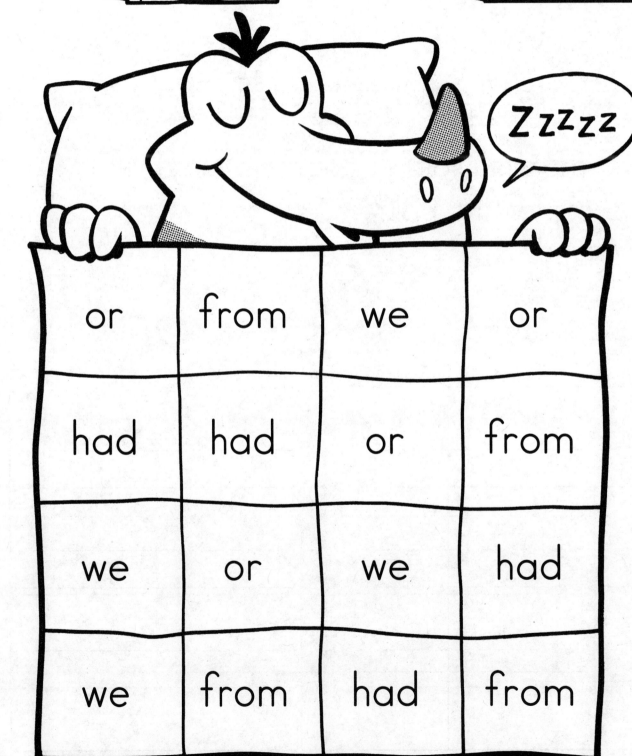 red

we yellow

from blue

or green

or	from	we	or
had	had	or	from
we	or	we	had
we	from	had	from

58

Name: _____

Count and graph the sight words.

	had	**from**	**we**	**or**
4				
3				
2				
1				

Little Learner Packets: Sight Words © Scholastic Inc.

Name: _____

Draw lines to match the sight words.

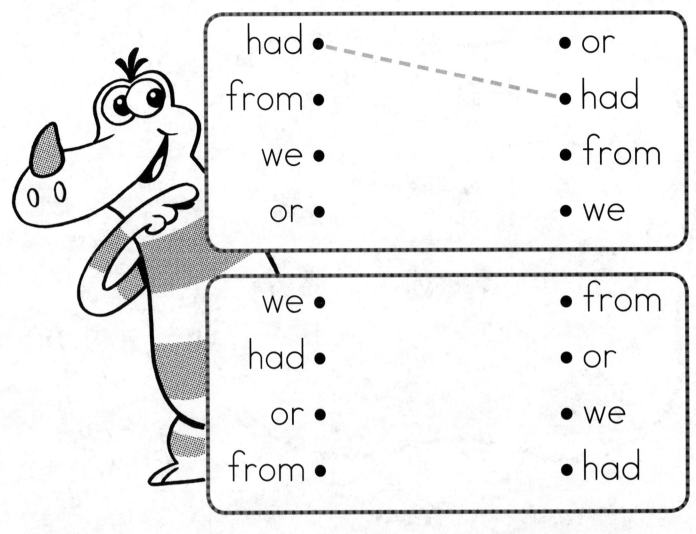

had •	• or
from •	• had
we •	• from
or •	• we

we •	• from
had •	• or
or •	• we
from •	• had

Circle each sight word from the Word Bank once.

```
k  j  v  c  o  r  y  l
f  g  u  x  f  r  o  m
m  w  e  n  a  l  i  w
s  u  r  i  h  a  d  o
```

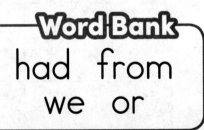

Word Bank

had from
we   or

Name: _____

Unscramble each sight word.

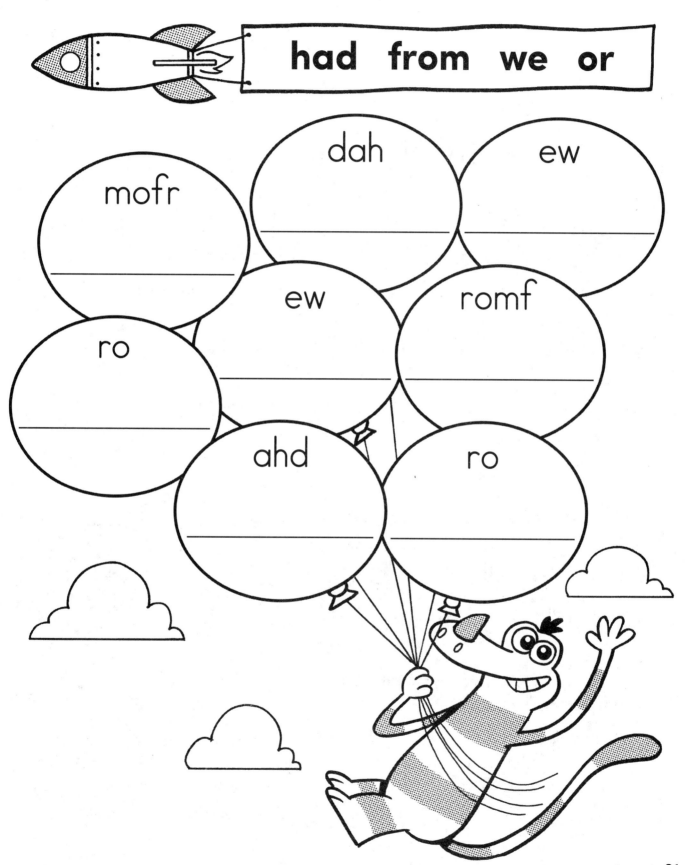

had   from   we   or

mofr
_____

dah
_____

ew
_____

ro
_____

ew
_____

romf
_____

ahd
_____

ro
_____

Word Bank

had

from

we

or

Use each sight word once to complete the story. Then read it aloud.

The monster had a friend _____ Mars.

"I think _____ should fly to my planet,"
said the friend.

The friend _____ two spaceships.

"Want to go in the big one _____
the small one?" he asked.

**Color the boxes with the four sight words
you learned in this packet.**

is	we	or	of
from	a	in	had

BYE!
GREAT
JOB!

Little Learner Packets: Sight Words © Scholastic Inc.

Name: _____

SIGHT WORDS
said, words
not, what

Hi!

said said

words words

not not

what what

Write the words above. Color in each box when you complete an activity.

① Introduction	② Read & Write	③ Read & Write	④ Color
⑤ Graph	⑥ Match & Find	⑦ Unscramble	⑧ Review

Name: _____

Read the sentence.

The ghost **<u>said</u>** the **<u>words</u>**, "I am very scary!"

Write the sight words.

said

words

Name: _____

Read the sentence.

He said, "Guess **what**? I am **not** really a ghost!"

Write the sight words.

what

~~what~~

----

not

~~not~~

Name: _____

Use the code to color the sight words.

said  red

not yellow

words blue

what green

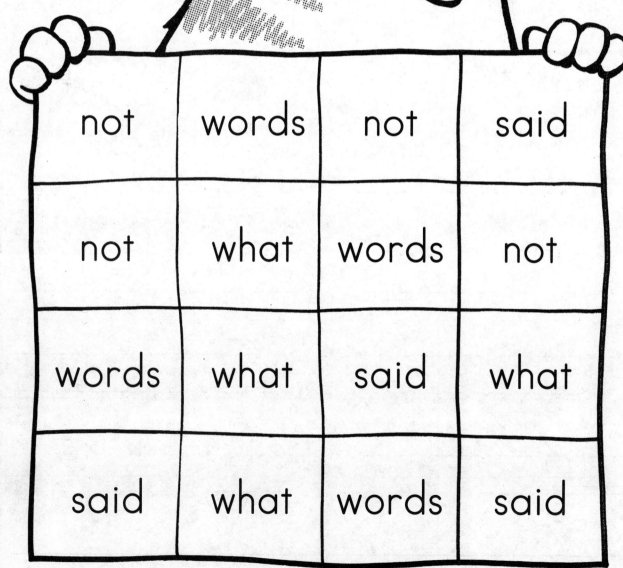

Zzzz

not	words	not	said
not	what	words	not
words	what	said	what
said	what	words	said

Little Learner Packets: Sight Words © Scholastic Inc.

Name: _____

Count and graph the sight words.

	said	words	not	what
4				
3				
2				
1				

Little Learner Packets: Sight Words © Scholastic Inc.

Name: _____

Draw lines to match the sight words.

said •   • what

words •   • words

not •   • said

what •   • not

words •   • not

what •   • what

not •   • said

said •   • words

Circle each sight word from the Word Bank once.

d s p w h a t n

t y z s a i d r

x l m n o t p a

a w o r d s e j

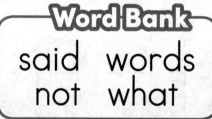

Word Bank

said   words
not   what

Little Learner Packets: Sight Words © Scholastic Inc.

Name: _____

Unscramble each sight word.

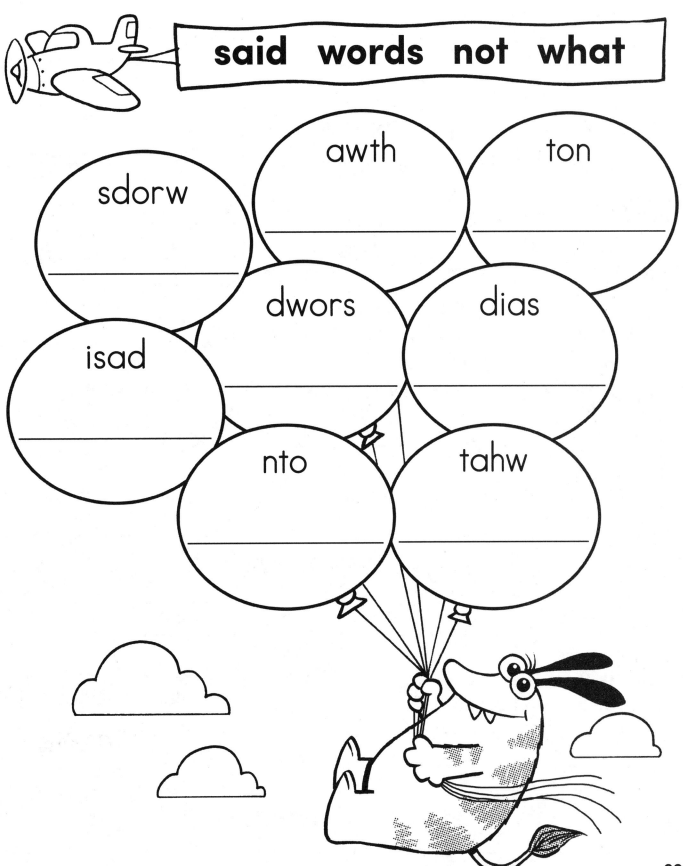

said words not what

sdorw
_____

awth
_____

ton
_____

dwors
_____

dias
_____

isad
_____

nto
_____

tahw
_____

Name: _____

A Poem for My Pal

A ghost is scary.

A ghost says, "Boo!"

Are you a ghost?

No, you are just you!

Word Bank

said

words

not

what

Use each sight word once to complete the story. Then read it aloud.

The monster wrote _____ on paper.

But he did _____ write a story.

So _____ did the monster write?

"I wrote a poem for my pal!" he _____.

Color the boxes with the four sight words you learned in this packet.

the	a	not	by
said	words	is	what

BYE! GREAT JOB!

Little Learner Packets: Sight Words © Scholastic Inc.

Name: _____

SIGHT WORDS
all, were, can, by

Hi!

all all _____

were were _____

can can _____

by by _____

Write the words above. Color in each box when you complete an activity.

①	②	③	④
Introduction	**Read & Write**	**Read & Write**	**Color**
⑤	⑥	⑦	⑧
Graph	**Match & Find**	**Unscramble**	**Review**

Name: _____

Read the sentence.

Wow, **all** of the monsters **were** at the party!

Write the sight words.

all

were

Name: _____

Read the sentence.

The monster <u>can</u> dance <u>by</u> the band.

Write the sight words.

can

by

Name: _____

Use the code to color the sight words.

all ⟨ red ⟩

can ⟨ yellow ⟩

were ⟨ blue ⟩

by ⟨ green ⟩

Zzzz

by	can	by	can
were	all	can	all
can	by	were	by
were	all	all	were

Count and graph the sight words.

	all	**were**	**can**	**by**
4				
3				
2				
1				

Name: _____

Draw lines to match the sight words.

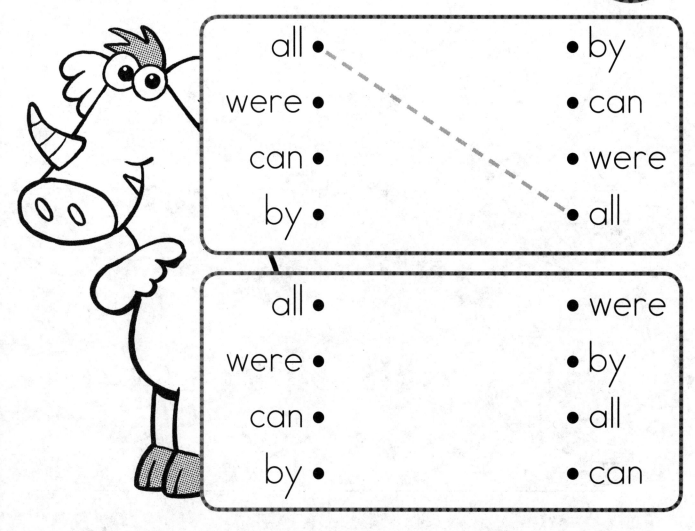

all •   • by

were •   • can

can •   • were

by •   • all

all •   • were

were •   • by

can •   • all

by •   • can

Circle each sight word from the Word Bank once.

l u z b y p o n

s d i w c a n c

p v a l l d s k

f r w e r e w o

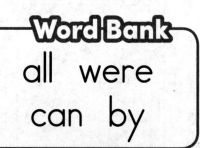

Word Bank

all   were

can   by

Little Learner Packets: Sight Words © Scholastic Inc.

Name: _____

Unscramble each sight word.

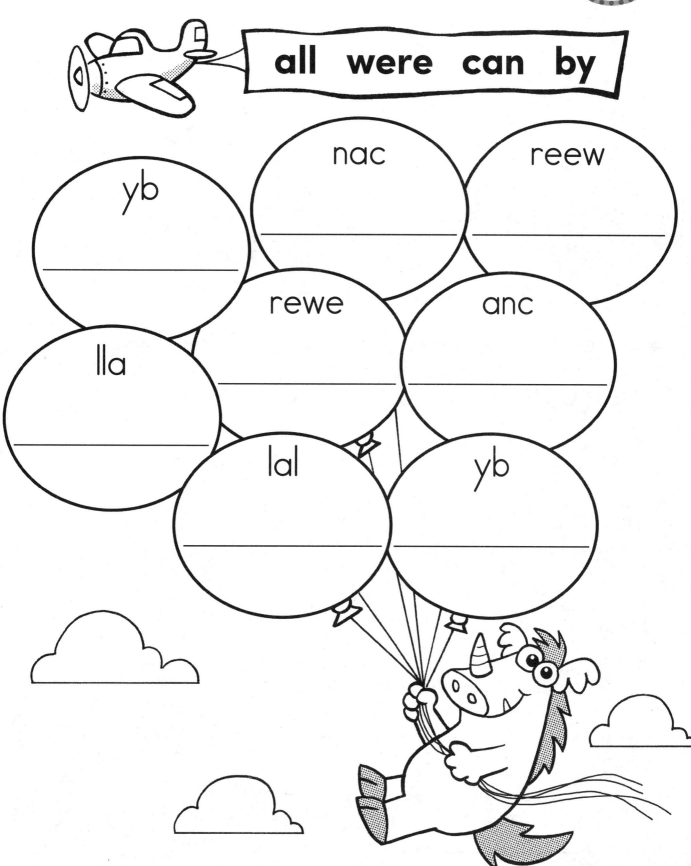

all   were   can   by

yb
_____

nac
_____

reew
_____

rewe
_____

anc
_____

lla
_____

lal
_____

yb
_____

Name: _____

Word Bank

all

were

can

by

Use each sight word once to complete the story. Then read it aloud.

The monsters _____ at the birthday party.

They stood _____ a very big cake.

The little monster blew out _____ of her candles.

"Now everyone _____ have cake!" she said.

Color the boxes with the four sight words you learned in this packet.

all	a	can	by
said	the	of	were

BYE! GREAT JOB!

SIGHT WORDS
but, one,
when, your

Hi!

but   but

one   one

when   when

your   your

Write the words above. Color in each box when you complete an activity.

① Introduction	② Read & Write	③ Read & Write	④ Color
⑤ Graph	⑥ Match & Find	⑦ Unscramble	⑧ Review

Name: _____

Read the sentence.

There were two friends, **but** only **one** cookie.

Write the sight words.

but	one
b̶u̶t̶	o̶n̶e̶

Little Learner Packets: Sight Words © Scholastic Inc.

Name: _____

Read the sentence.

"I was happy **when** you decided to share **your** cookie with me," said the robot.

Write the sight words.

when

your

Name: _____

Use the code to color the sight words.

but  red

when yellow

one blue

your green

Zzzz

when	one	when	but
but	your	one	your
when	but	when	one
but	your	one	your

Name: _____

Count and graph the sight words.

	but	one	when	your
4				
3				
2				
1				

Name: _____

Draw lines to match the sight words.

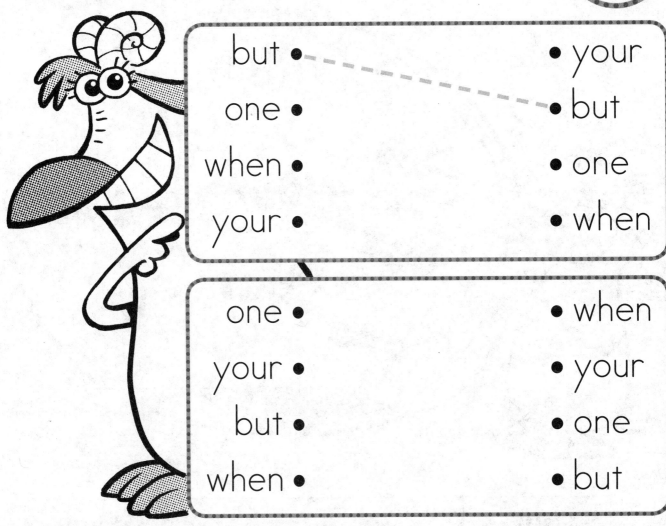

but •   • your

one •   • but

when •   • one

your •   • when

one •   • when

your •   • your

but •   • one

when •   • but

Circle each sight word from the Word Bank once.

f g y o u r x o

s o n e r a c i

y p a f w h e n

h v a b u t o r

Word Bank

but   one
when   your

Little Learner Packets: Sight Words © Scholastic Inc.

Name: _____

Unscramble each sight word.

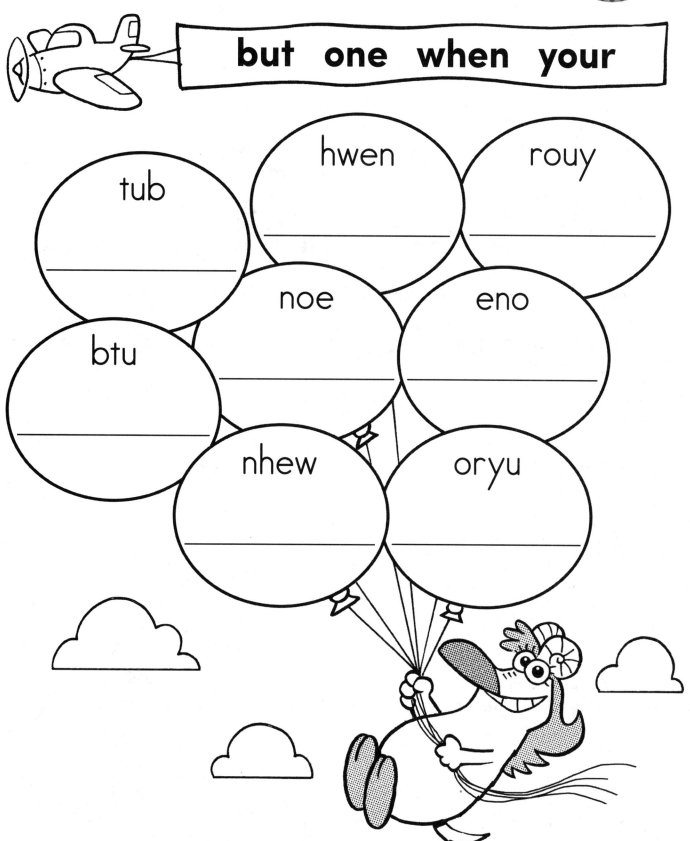

but   one   when   your

tub

_____

hwen

_____

rouy

_____

btu

_____

noe

_____

eno

_____

nhew

_____

oryu

_____

Name: _____

Word Bank

but

one

when

your

Use each sight word once to complete the story. Then read it aloud.

The monster got a ball _____ he went to the mall.

"I love _____ new ball!" said the robot.

I like it, _____ I want you to have it," said the monster.

"Thanks! You are _____ great pal!" said the robot.

Color the boxes with the four sight words you learned in this packet.

but	we	when	of
you	one	in	your

BYE! GREAT JOB!

Little Learner Packets: Sight Words © Scholastic Inc.

Answer Key

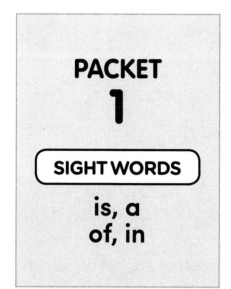

PACKET 1

SIGHT WORDS

is, a
of, in

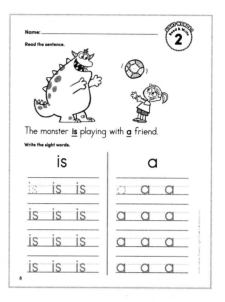

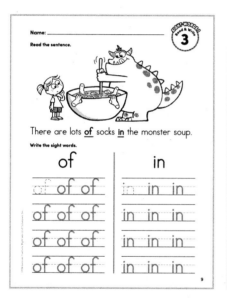

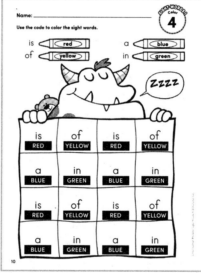

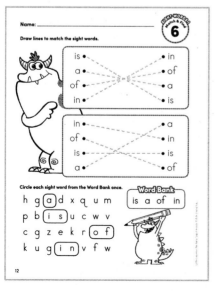

PACKET 2

SIGHT WORDS

and, the
to, you

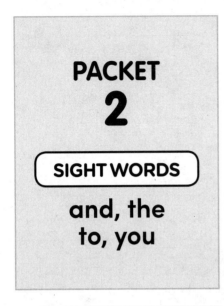

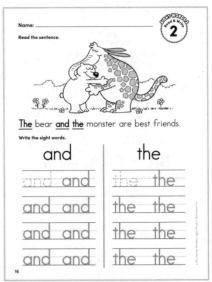

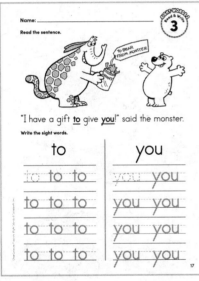

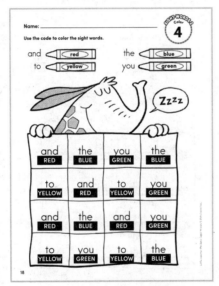

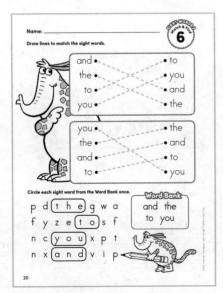

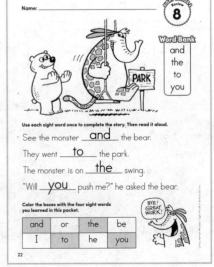

PACKET 3

SIGHT WORDS

that, it
he, was

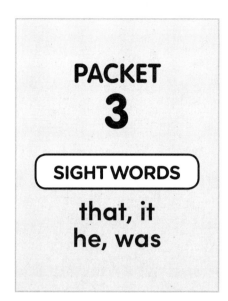

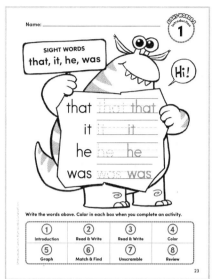

SIGHT WORDS
that, it, he, was

Hi!

that   that that
it   it   it
he   he   he
was   was was

Write the words above. Color in each box when you complete an activity.

| ① Introduction | ② Read & Write | ③ Read & Write | ④ Color |
| ⑤ Graph | ⑥ Match & Find | ⑦ Unscramble | ⑧ Review |

23

Read the sentence.

The monster was sad **that it** was raining.

Write the sight words.

that	it
that that	it it
that that	it it
that that	it it
that that	it it

24

Read the sentence.

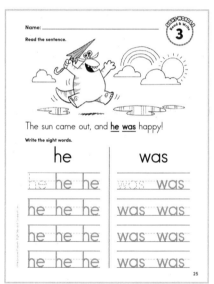

The sun came out, and **he was** happy!

Write the sight words.

he	was
he he he	was was
he he he	was was
he he he	was was
he he he	was was

25

Use the code to color the sight words.

that — red   it — blue
he — yellow   was — green

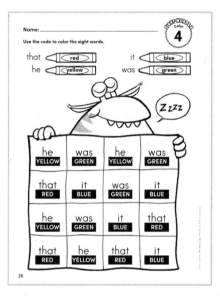

Zzzz

he YELLOW	was GREEN	he YELLOW	was GREEN
that RED	it BLUE	was GREEN	it BLUE
he YELLOW	was GREEN	it BLUE	that RED
that RED	he YELLOW	that RED	it BLUE

26

Count and graph the sight words.

that   it   it
he   was
was   that   it
it   was

	that	it	he	was
4				
3				
2				
1				

27

Draw lines to match the sight words.

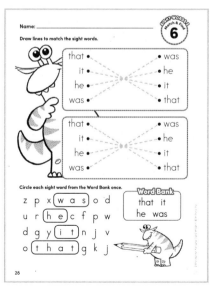

that • • was
it • • he
he • • it
was • • that

that • • was
it • • he
he • • it
was • • that

Circle each sight word from the Word Bank once.

z p x w a s o d
u r h e c f p w
d g y i t n j v
o t h a t g k j

Word Bank
that it
he was

28

Unscramble each sight word.

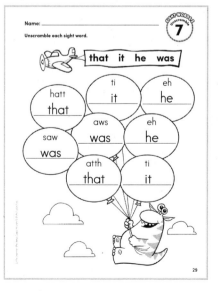

that it he was

hatt — that
ti — it
eh — he
saw — was
aws — was
eh — he
atth — that
ti — it

29

HELLO, BIG FISH!

Word Bank
that
it
he
was

Use each sight word once to complete the story. Then read it aloud.

The monster ___was___ at the beach.

He saw ___that___ big fish.

He saw ___it___ jump up and wave.

So ___he___ said, "Hello, big fish!"

BYE! GREAT JOB!

Color the boxes with the four sight words you learned in this packet.

not	it	the	that
was	he	can	said

30

PACKET 4

SIGHT WORDS

she, for are, as

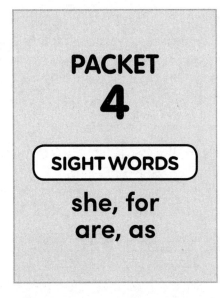

SIGHT WORDS
she, for, are, as

she   she she
for   for for
are   are are
as   as   as

Write the words above. Color in each box when you complete an activity.

| ① Introduction | ② Read & Write | ③ Read & Write | ④ Color |
| ⑤ Graph | ⑥ Match & Find | ⑦ Unscramble | ⑧ Review |

31

Read the sentence.

Look, **she** has a teddy bear **for** the baby!

Write the sight words.

she
she she
she she
she she
she she

for
for for
for for
for for
for for

32

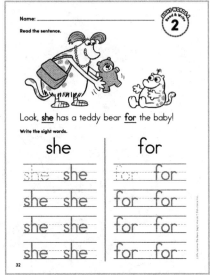

Read the sentence.

The cats **are** **as** sleepy **as** the baby monster.

Write the sight words.

are
are are
are are
are are
are are

as
as as as
as as as
as as as
as as as

33

Use the code to color the sight words.

she → red   for → blue
are → yellow as → green

are YELLOW	as GREEN	for BLUE	as GREEN
she RED	for BLUE	she RED	are YELLOW
she RED	are YELLOW	as GREEN	as GREEN
are YELLOW	for BLUE	she RED	for BLUE

34

Count and graph the sight words.

she as are
are for as
are as she
as are

	she	for	are	as
4				
3				
2				
1				

35

Draw lines to match the sight words.

she —— for
for —— as
are —— are
as —— she

as —— as
are —— for
for —— she
she —— are

Circle each sight word from the Word Bank once.

t g s h e b v o
v u f o r n g m
r u c d a s r i
c o p o t a r e

Word Bank
she for
are as

36

Unscramble each sight word.

she for are as

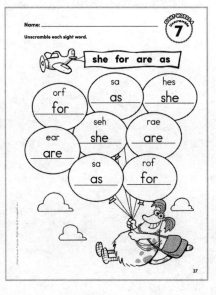

orf
for

sa
as

hes
she

seh
she

rae
are

ear
are

sa
as

rof
for

37

Word Bank
she
for
are
as

Use each sight word once to complete the story. Then read it aloud.

Here ___are___ two nice monsters.

He is a baby, and ___she___ is a mom.

She has a bottle ___for___ the baby.

He is ___as___ happy as can be!

Color the boxes with the four sight words you learned in this packet.

| a | for | by | are |
| is | as | said | she |

38

90

PACKET 5

SIGHT WORDS

I, on
they, with

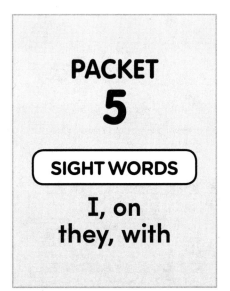

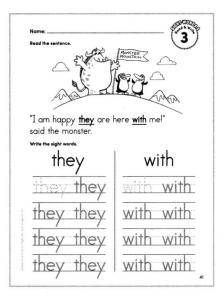

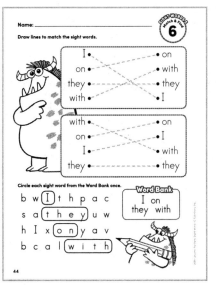

PACKET 6

SIGHT WORDS

be, at have, this

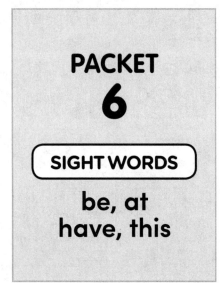

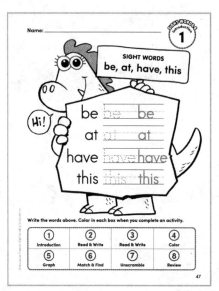

Name: _____

1 SIGHT WORDS Introduction

Hi!

SIGHT WORDS
be, at, have, this

be | be | be
at | at | at
have | have | have
this | this | this

Write the words above. Color in each box when you complete an activity.

| ① Introduction | ② Read & Write | ③ Read & Write | ④ Color |
| ⑤ Graph | ⑥ Match & Find | ⑦ Unscramble | ⑧ Review |

47

Name: _____

2 SIGHT WORDS Read & Write

Read the sentence.

HAT SHOP

The monster loves to **be at** the hat shop!

Write the sight words.

be | **at**

be be be	at at at
be be be	at at at
be be be	at at at
be be be	at at at

48

Name: _____

3 SIGHT WORDS Read & Write

Read the sentence.

"I **have** to try on **this** tall hat!" said the monster.

Write the sight words.

have | **this**

have have	this this
have have	this this
have have	this this
have have	this this

49

Name: _____

4 SIGHT WORDS Color

Use the code to color the sight words.

be — red | at — blue
have — yellow | this — green

have YELLOW	this GREEN	have YELLOW	this GREEN
be RED	at BLUE	at BLUE	be RED
have YELLOW	this GREEN	at BLUE	have YELLOW
be RED	at BLUE	be RED	this GREEN

50

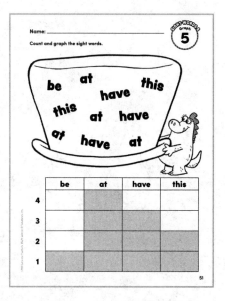

Name: _____

5 SIGHT WORDS Graph

Count and graph the sight words.

be at this
this have
this at have
at have at

	be	at	have	this
4				
3				
2				
1				

51

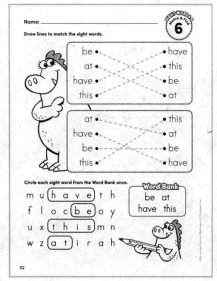

Name: _____

6 SIGHT WORDS Match & Find

Draw lines to match the sight words.

be • | • have
at • | • this
have • | • be
this • | • at

at • | • this
have • | • at
be • | • be
this • | • have

Circle each sight word from the Word Bank once.

m u h a v e t h
f l o c b e o y
u x t h i s m n
w z a t i r a h

Word Bank
be at
have this

52

Name: _____

7 SIGHT WORDS Unscramble

Unscramble each sight word.

be at have this

ta — at
eb — be
hits — this
vahe — have
eb — be
isht — this
ta — at
eavh — have

53

Name: _____

8 SIGHT WORDS Review

Word Bank
be
at
have
this

Use each sight word once to complete the story. Then read it aloud.

The monster was ___at___ the hat shop.

She put on ___this___ nice hat with dots.

The hat made her as happy as can ___be___

"I must ___have___ it!" she said.

BYE! GREAT JOB!

Color the boxes with the four sight words you learned in this packet.

| be | and | on | at |
| the | this | have | is |

54

92

PACKET 7

SIGHT WORDS

had, from
we, or

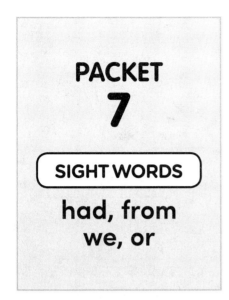

SIGHT WORDS
had, from, we, or

had   had had
from   from from
we   we   we
or   or   or

Hi!

Write the words above. Color in each box when you complete an activity.

① Introduction	② Read & Write	③ Read & Write	④ Color
⑤ Graph	⑥ Match & Find	⑦ Unscramble	⑧ Review

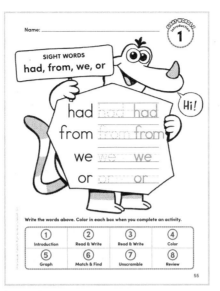

55

Name: ___

Read the sentence.

The monster **had** a pal **from** Mars.

Write the sight words.

had	from
had had	from from
had had	from from
had had	from from
had had	from from

56

Name: ___

Read the sentence.

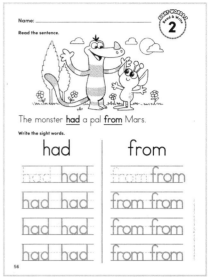

The monster said, "Should **we** play with the car **or** the ball?"

Write the sight words.

we	or
we we we	or or or
we we we	or or or
we we we	or or or
we we we	or or or

57

Name: ___

Use the code to color the sight words.

had → red   from → blue
we → yellow   or → green

or GREEN	from BLUE	we YELLOW	or GREEN
had RED	had RED	or GREEN	from BLUE
we YELLOW	or GREEN	we YELLOW	had RED
we YELLOW	from BLUE	had RED	from BLUE

Zzzzz

58

Name: ___

Count and graph the sight words.

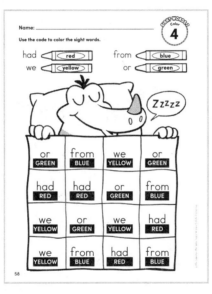

we from
had we or
or had we
we had

	had	from	we	or
4				
3				
2				
1				

59

Name: ___

Draw lines to match the sight words.

had •   • or
from •   • had
we •   • from
or •   • we

we •   • from
had •   • or
or •   • we
from •   • had

Circle each sight word from the Word Bank once.

k j v c o r y l
f g u x f r o m
m w e n a l i w
s u r i h a d o

Word Bank
had from
we or

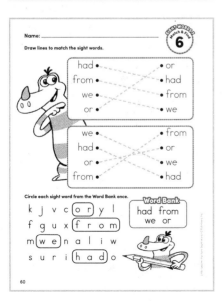

60

Name: ___

Unscramble each sight word.

had from we or

mofr → from
dah → had
ew → we
ro → or
ew → we
romf → from
ahd → had
ro → or

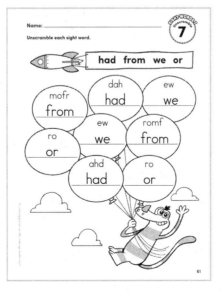

61

Name: ___

Word Bank
had
from
we
or

Use each sight word once to complete the story. Then read it aloud.

The monster had a friend **from** Mars.

"I think **we** should fly to my planet," said the friend.

The friend **had** two spaceships.

"Want to go in the big one **or** the small one?" he asked.

BYE! GREAT JOB!

Color the boxes with the four sight words you learned in this packet.

is	we	or	of
from	a	in	had

62

PACKET 8

SIGHT WORDS

said, words
not, what

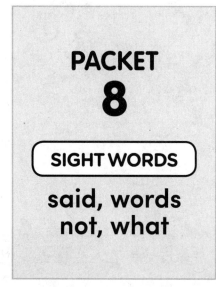

SIGHT WORDS
said, words
not, what

Hi!

said   said   said
words   words   words
not   not   not
what   what   what

Write the words above. Color in each box when you complete an activity.

| ① Introduction | ② Read & Write | ③ Read & Write | ④ Color |
| ⑤ Graph | ⑥ Match & Find | ⑦ Unscramble | ⑧ Review |

63

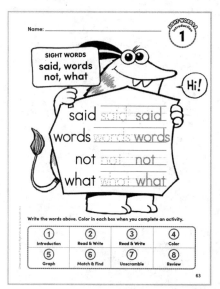

Name: _____

Read the sentence.

The ghost **said** the **words**, "I am very scary!"

Write the sight words.

said	words
said said	words
said said	words
said said	words
said said	words

64

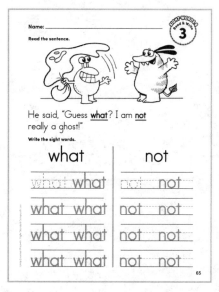

Name: _____

Read the sentence.

He **said**, "Guess **what**? I am **not** really a ghost!"

Write the sight words.

what	not
what what	not not
what what	not not
what what	not not
what what	not not

65

Name: _____

Use the code to color the sight words.

said — red   words — blue
not — yellow   what — green

Zzzz

not YELLOW	words BLUE	not YELLOW	said RED
not YELLOW	what GREEN	words BLUE	not YELLOW
words BLUE	what GREEN	said RED	what GREEN
said RED	what GREEN	words BLUE	said RED

66

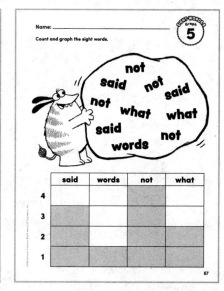

Name: _____

Count and graph the sight words.

not said not said
not what what
said not
words

	said	words	not	what
4				
3				
2				
1				

67

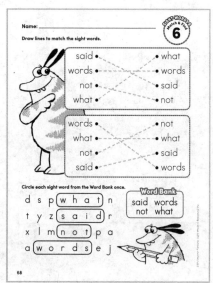

Name: _____

Draw lines to match the sight words.

said • — • what
words • — • words
not • — • said
what • — • not

words • — • not
what • — • what
not • — • said
said • — • words

Circle each sight word from the Word Bank once.

d s p [w h a t] n
t y z [s a i d] r
x l m [n o t] p a
a [w o r d s] e j

Word Bank
said words
not what

68

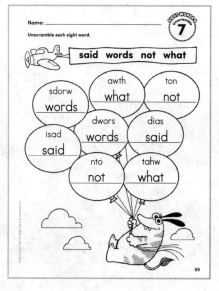

Name: _____

Unscramble each sight word.

said words not what

sdorw → words
awth → what
ton → not
isad → said
dwors → words
dias → said
nto → not
tahw → what

69

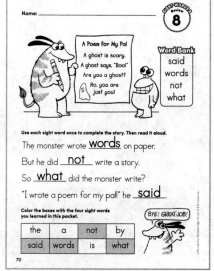

Name: _____

A Poem for My Pal
A ghost is scary.
A ghost says, "Boo!"
Are you a ghost?
No, you are just you!

Word Bank
said
words
not
what

Use each sight word once to complete the story. Then read it aloud.

The monster wrote **words** on paper.

But he did **not** write a story.

So **what** did the monster write?

"I wrote a poem for my pal!" he **said**

Color the boxes with the four sight words you learned in this packet.

the	a	not	by
said	words	is	what

BYE! GREAT JOB!

70

PACKET 9

SIGHT WORDS

all, were
can, by

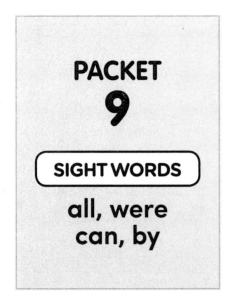

Name: _____

SIGHT WORDS
all, were, can, by

Hi!

all	all	all
were	were	were
can	can	can
by	by	by

Write the words above. Color in each box when you complete an activity.

| ① Introduction | ② Read & Write | ③ Read & Write | ④ Color |
| ⑤ Graph | ⑥ Match & Find | ⑦ Unscramble | ⑧ Review |

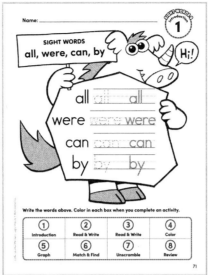

71

Name: _____

Read the sentence.

BIRTHDAY PARTY!

Wow, **all** of the monsters **were** at the party!

Write the sight words.

all	were
all all all	were were
all all all	were were
all all all	were were
all all all	were were

72

Name: _____

Read the sentence.

The monster **can** dance **by** the band.

Write the sight words.

can	by
can can	by by by
can can	by by by
can can	by by by
can can	by by by

73

Name: _____

Use the code to color the sight words.

all — red   were — blue
can — yellow   by — green

Zzzz

by GREEN	can YELLOW	by GREEN	can YELLOW
were BLUE	all RED	can YELLOW	all RED
can YELLOW	by GREEN	were BLUE	by GREEN
were BLUE	all RED	all RED	were BLUE

74

Name: _____

Count and graph the sight words.

can   all
all   were   can
were   all   by
all   can

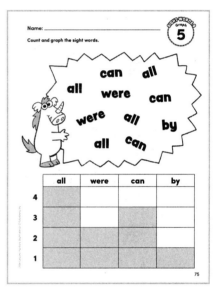

	all	were	can	by
4				
3				
2				
1				

75

Name: _____

6

Draw lines to match the sight words.

all • • by
were • • can
can • • were
by • • all

all • • were
were • • by
can • • all
by • • can

Circle each sight word from the Word Bank once.

l u z **by** p o n
s d i w **can** c
p v **all** d s k
f r **were** w o

Word Bank
all were
can by

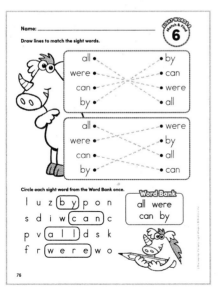

76

Name: _____

7

Unscramble each sight word.

all were can by

yb — **by**
nac — **can**
reew — **were**
rewe — **were**
anc — **can**
lla — **all**
lal — **all**
yb — **by**

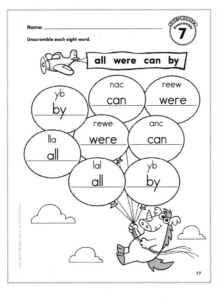

77

Name: _____

HAPPY BIRTHDAY!

Word Bank
all
were
can
by

Use each sight word once to complete the story. Then read it aloud.

The monsters **were** at the birthday party.

They stood **by** a very big cake.

The little monster blew out **all**
of her candles.

"Now everyone **can** have cake!" she said.

Color the boxes with the four sight words
you learned in this packet.

all	a	can	by
said	the	of	were

BYE! GREAT JOB!

78

PACKET 10

SIGHT WORDS

but, one
when, your

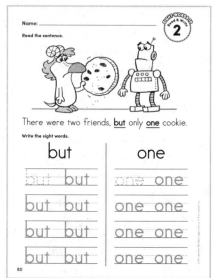

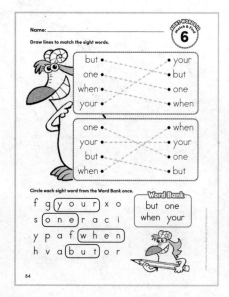